The Ultimate Self-Teaching Method!

Play Recorder Today!

PLAYBACK+
Speed · Pitch · Balance · Loop

To access audio visit:
www.halleonard.com/mylibrary
Enter Code
6414-2211-8066-7352

A Complete Guide to the Basics

Contents

Editor and Recording Producer:
Tom Anderson

Introduction

Welcome to *Play Recorder Today!*—the series designed to prepare you for any style of recorder playing, from rock to blues to jazz to classical. Whatever your taste in music, *Play Recorder Today!* will give you the start you need.

About the Audio

It's easy and fun to play recorder, and the accompanying audio will make your learning even more enjoyable, as we take you step by step through each lesson and play each song along with a full band. Much as a real lesson, the best way to learn this material is to read and practice a while first on your own, then listen to the audio. With *Play Recorder Today!*, you can learn at your own pace. If there is ever something that you don't quite understand the first time through, go back and listen again. Every musical track has been given a track number, so if you want to practice a song again, you can find it right away.

ISBN 978-1-4234-6138-8

HAL•LEONARD®

Visit Hal Leonard Online at
www.halleonard.com

Contact Us:
Hal Leonard
7777 West Bluemound Road
Milwaukee, WI 53213
Email: info@halleonard.com

In Europe contact:
Hal Leonard Europe Limited
42 Wigmore Street
Marylebone, London, W1U 2RN
Email: info@halleonardeurope.com

In Australia contact:
Hal Leonard Australia Pty. Ltd.
4 Lentara Court
Cheltenham, Victoria, 3192 Australia
Email: info@halleonard.com.au

The Basics

The Parts of the Recorder

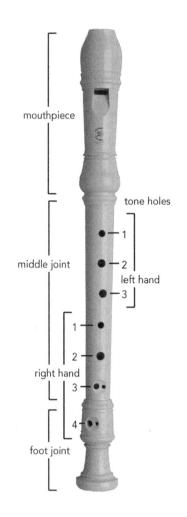

Assembling Your Recorder

- Most recorders come fully assembled.
- You can separate the mouth piece, middle joint and foot joint for cleaning.
- If your recorder is in three pieces, assemble it to look like the picture to the right.

Posture

Whether sitting on the edge of your chair or standing, you should always keep your:

- Spine straight and tall,
- Shoulders back and relaxed, and
- Feet flat on the floor.

Breathing and Tone Flow

The natural tone of the recorder is sweet, clear and steady. The air you use must flow slowly and remain constant. Never blow hard.

- Place the palm of your hand near your mouth.
- Pretend to take a "drink" of air, filling your belly.
- Let the air out slowly and steadily against your palm like blowing soup in a spoon to cool it down.
- Do the same but pretend to say "doo(d)." Hold on to the vowel sound "oo." Make the final "d" very soft.

The air you feel is the air stream. It produces sound through the instrument. Your tongue is like a faucet or valve that releases the air stream.

Your First Tone

Tone is musical sound. On the recorder you do not want it to be shrill or harsh. Follow these steps to practice making a tone:

- Hold the instrument below the vent opening under the mouthpiece with one hand.
- Put the mouthpiece between your lips in front of your teeth. "Drink in" with air and pretend to say "doo(d)."
- Hold on to the "oo" sound and end with a soft "d."
- Check that you are using a steady stream of air and that you are not over blowing.

How to Hold Your Recorder

The fingers on your left and right hands are numbered.

- Relax both hands. Stack your hands so the left hand is on top.
- Take the recorder and place your left thumb on the hole in the back of the instrument.
- Place the 1st, 2nd and 3rd fingers of your left hand over the top three holes.
- Place the 1st, 2nd, 3rd and 4th fingers of your right hand over the bottom four sets of holes (the lowest sets of holes are pairs of two each).
- Do not blow into the recorder yet. Practice moving your fingers to see if you are covering the holes.

Putting Away Your Instrument

- Carefully shake any condensation out of your instrument.
- Using the cleaning rod, run a soft, clean cloth into the mouthpiece and through the middle and foot joints.
- The mouthpiece can be cleaned in warm, soapy water then rinsed in warm, clear water.

Reading Music

Musical sounds are indicated by symbols called **notes** written on a **staff**. Notes come in several forms, but every note indicates **pitch** and **rhythm**.

The Staff

Music Staff

The **music staff** has 5 lines and 4 spaces where notes and rests are written.

Ledger Lines

Ledger lines extend the music staff. Notes on ledger lines can be above or below the staff.

Measures & Bar Lines

Measure Measure

Bar Line Bar Line Double Bar Line

Bar lines divide the music staff into **measures**. The **double bar** indicates the end of a piece of music.

Treble Clef
(G Clef) indicates the position of note names on a music staff: Second line is G.

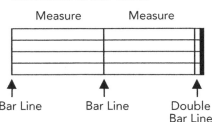

Time Signature
indicates how many beats per measure and what kind of note gets one beat.

= **4 beats** per measure
= **Quarter note** gets one beat

Pitch

Pitch (the highness or lowness of a note) is indicated by the horizontal placement of the note on the staff. Notes higher on the staff are higher in pitch; notes lower on the staff are lower in pitch. To name the pitches, we use the first seven letters of the alphabet: A, B, C, D, E, F, and G. The **treble clef** (𝄞) assigns a particular pitch name to each line and space on the staff, centered around the pitch G, located on the second line of the staff. Music for the recorder is always written in the treble clef. (Some instruments may make use of other clefs, which make the lines and spaces represent different pitches.)

Note Names

Each note is on a line or space of the staff. These note names are indicated by the treble clef.

Sharps, Flats, and Naturals

These musical symbols sometimes called "accidentals" raise or lower the pitch of a note.

Sharp ♯ raises the note and remains in effect for the entire measure.

Flat ♭ lowers the note and remains in effect for the entire measure.

Natural ♮ cancels a flat (♭) or sharp (♯) and remains in effect for the entire measure.

Rhythm

Rhythm refers to how long or for how many **beats** a note lasts. The beat is the pulse of music, and like your heartbeat it usually remains very steady. To help keep track of the beats in a piece of music, the staff is divided into **measures**. The **time signature** (numbers such as $\frac{4}{4}$ or $\frac{6}{8}$ at the beginning of the staff) indicates how many beats you will find in each measure. Counting the beats or tapping your foot can help to maintain a steady beat. Tap your foot down on each beat and up on each "&,"

$\frac{4}{4}$ Time

Count:	1	&	2	&	3	&	4	&
Tap:	↓	↑	↓	↑	↓	↑	↓	↑

$\frac{4}{4}$ is probably the most common time signature. The **top number** tells you how many beats are in each measure; the **bottom number** tells you what kind of note receives one beat. In $\frac{4}{4}$ time there are four beats in the measure and a **quarter note** (♩ or ♪) equals one beat.

---

4 = **4 beats** per measure
4 = **Quarter note** gets one beat

The First Note: B

To play "B," place your finger and thumb on the holes as shown. The holes that are colored in should be covered.

Notes and Rests

Music uses symbols to indicate both the length of sound and of silence. Symbols indicating sound are called **notes**. Symbols indicating silence are called **rests**.

Quarter Note/Quarter Rest

A quarter note means to play for one full beat. A quarter rest means to be silent for one full beat. There are four quarter notes or quarter rests in a $\frac{4}{4}$ measure.

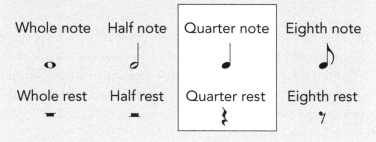

Each note should begin with the sound "doo" to help separate it from the others.

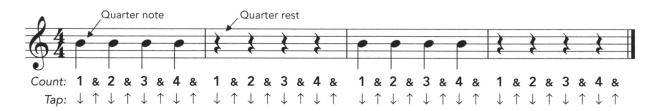

Count: 1 & 2 & 3 & 4 &   1 & 2 & 3 & 4 &   1 & 2 & 3 & 4 &   1 & 2 & 3 & 4 &
Tap: ↓ ↑ ↓ ↑ ↓ ↑ ↓ ↑   ↓ ↑ ↓ ↑ ↓ ↑ ↓ ↑   ↓ ↑ ↓ ↑ ↓ ↑ ↓ ↑   ↓ ↑ ↓ ↑ ↓ ↑ ↓ ↑

A New Note: A

Look at the fingering diagram beside each new note. Repeat each exercise several times until you feel comfortable playing the new notes.

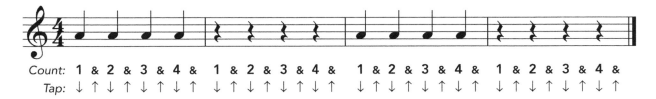

Count: **1 & 2 & 3 & 4 &   1 & 2 & 3 & 4 &   1 & 2 & 3 & 4 &   1 & 2 & 3 & 4 &**
Tap: ↓ ↑ ↓ ↑ ↓ ↑ ↓ ↑ ↓ ↑ ↓ ↑ ↓ ↑ ↓ ↑ ↓ ↑ ↓ ↑ ↓ ↑ ↓ ↑ ↓ ↑ ↓ ↑ ↓ ↑ ↓ ↑

Don't just let the audio play on. Repeat each exercise until you feel comfortable playing it by yourself and with the recording.

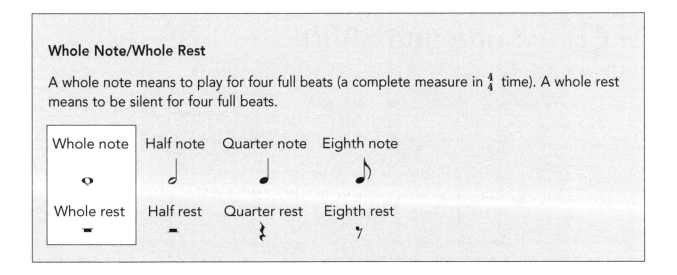

Whole Note/Whole Rest

A whole note means to play for four full beats (a complete measure in $\frac{4}{4}$ time). A whole rest means to be silent for four full beats.

Whole note	Half note	Quarter note	Eighth note
𝅝	𝅗𝅥	𝅘𝅥	𝅘𝅥𝅮
Whole rest	Half rest	Quarter rest	Eighth rest
—	—	𝄽	𝄾

Moving Down

Play each whole note with a long, sustained "doo" sound. Count four silent beats for each whole rest.

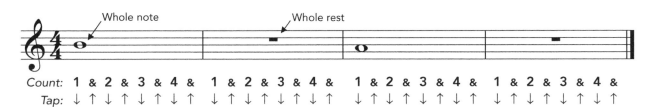

Whole note   Whole rest

Count: **1 & 2 & 3 & 4 &   1 & 2 & 3 & 4 &   1 & 2 & 3 & 4 &   1 & 2 & 3 & 4 &**
Tap: ↓ ↑ ↓ ↑ ↓ ↑ ↓ ↑ ↓ ↑ ↓ ↑ ↓ ↑ ↓ ↑ ↓ ↑ ↓ ↑ ↓ ↑ ↓ ↑ ↓ ↑ ↓ ↑ ↓ ↑ ↓ ↑

Track 4

Down and Up

Now you are ready to play quarter notes and whole notes. Make sure you sustain the sound of each note using good breath support.

Count/ **1** & **2** & **3** & **4** & **1** & **2** & **3** & **4** & **1** & **2** & **3** & **4** & **1** & **2** & **3** & **4** &
Tap:

Remember: Rests are silence in music where you play nothing at all. Rests are like notes in that they have their own rhythmic values, instructing you how long (or for how many beats) to pause. Here, four beats of rest can be simplified as a whole rest.

Track 5

Long and Short

Count/ **1** & **2** & **3** & **4** & **1** & **2** & **3** & **4** & **1** & **2** & **3** & **4** & **1** & **2** & **3** & **4** &
Tap:

Keeping Time

To keep a steady tempo, try tapping your foot and counting along with each song. In $\frac{4}{4}$ time, tap your foot four times in each measure and count, "1 & 2 & 3 & 4 &." Your foot should touch the floor on the number and come up on the "&." Each number and each "&" should be exactly the same duration, like the ticking of a clock.

Track 6

A New Note: G

Are you completely covering the first three holes on top as well as the thumb hole? The note "G" should sound lower than "A" or "B."

Count/ **1** & **2** & **3** & **4** & **1** & **2** & **3** & **4** & **1** & **2** & **3** & **4** & **1** & **2** & **3** & **4** &
Tap:

Putting It Together

Now you are ready to play "G," "A," and "B." Keep your left thumb covering the thumb hole. Do not lift your first three fingers very high when you are not covering the holes. Your fingers should remain curved when playing the recorder.

1 & 2 & 3 & 4 &   1 & 2 & 3 & 4 &   1 & 2 & 3 & 4 &   1 & 2 & 3 & 4 &

Rolling Along

Here is your first song. Playing recorder offers you many opportunities to play well-known melodies. This melody is eight measures long. Continue to the second line of music after you have completed the first line.

Continue to the next line

Tonguing

To start each note, whisper the syllable "doo." Keep the air stream going continuously and touch the tip of your tongue against your upper teeth for each new note. If the notes change, be sure to move your fingers quickly so that each note will come out cleanly. When you come to a rest or the end of the song, just stop blowing. Using your tongue to stop the air will cause an abrupt and unpleasant ending of the sound.

- Play long tones to warm up at the beginning of every practice session.
- Tap, count out loud, and sing through each exercise with the audio before you play it.
- Play each exercise several times until you feel comfortable with it.

Notes and Rests

Half Note/Half Rest

A half note means to play for two full beats. (It's equal in length to two quarter notes.) A half rest means to be silent for two beats. There are two half notes or half rests in a $\frac{4}{4}$ measure.

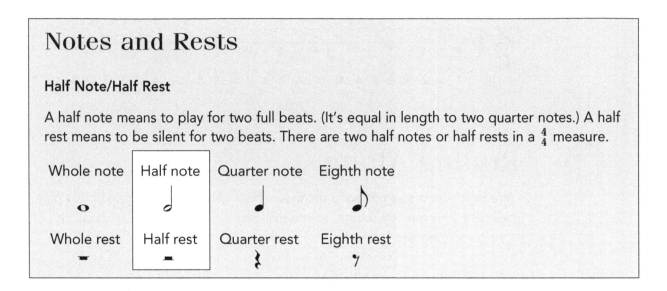

Track 9

Half Time Show

Track 10

Hot Cross Buns

If you become winded or dizzy you are probably blowing too hard. You can still practice by fingering the notes on your instrument and singing the pitches or counting the rhythm out loud.

Did you remember to continue from one line of music to the next? Most songs are written on more than one line. Look ahead to see how many lines of music are used. Anticipating when reading music is a good thing.

Repeat Signs

Repeat signs 𝄆 ╎ 𝄇 tell you to repeat everything between them. If only the sign on the right appears (:‖), repeat from the beginning of the piece.

Track 11

From the Top

Repeat sign →

Track 12

Once Again

Tempo Markings

The speed or pace of music is called **tempo**. Tempo markings are usually written above the staff. Many of these terms come from the Italian language.

Allegro	*(ah lay' grow)*	Fast tempo
Moderato	*(mah der ah' tow)*	Medium or moderate tempo
Andante	*(ahn dahn' tay)*	Slower "walking" tempo

Track 13

Au Claire de la Lune

Moderato

Did you observe the tempo marking and play at a medium tempo?

A Sense of Tempo

The speed of music is very important. Can you think of a song that makes you want to dance because of its fast, strong beat? Or is there a piece of classical music or well-known folk song that creates a somber mood because of its slow, steady beat? How fast you are playing is a primary element in music.

Breath Mark

The **breath mark** (,) indicates a specific place to inhale. Play the preceding note for the full length then take a deep, quick breath through your mouth.

Track 14

Suo Gan

Breath Support

In order to play in tune and with a full, beautiful tone, it is necessary to breathe properly and control the air as you play. Take the breath in through your mouth all the way to the bottom of your lungs. Slowly push the air through your lips creating a steady stream of air — much like blowing on a spoon of hot soup.

Do not over blow. This will cause high, unpleasant sounds to come out of your recorder. Even if a breath mark is not indicated, take a breath whenever needed to assist your breath support.

Dynamics

Dynamics refer to how loud or soft the music is. Traditionally, many musical terms (including dynamic markings) are called by their Italian names:

f   forte *(four' tay)*   loud
mf mezzo forte *(met' zoh four' tay)*   moderately loud
p   piano *(pee ahn' oh)*   soft

Track 15

Skipping Around

Do not over blow at the louder dynamic levels. Control your tone with a constant stream of air and good breath support.

- Keep your lips soft and relaxed.
- Keep your throat open and free from tension.
- Use a steady stream of air without over blowing.
- Have a relaxed tongue when starting notes.

Track 16

C to Shining C (New Note: C)

Always practice long tones on each new note.
This note is played with the middle finger and
thumb of your left hand.

C Scape

Track 17

Dynamic Changes

Gradual changes in volume are indicated by these symbols:

    Crescendo (gradually louder)   sometimes abbreviated *cresc.*

    Decrescendo or *Diminuendo* (gradually softer)   sometimes abbreviated *dim.*

Remember to keep the air stream moving fast both as you get louder by gradually using more air on the crescendo, *and* as you get softer by gradually using less air on the decrescendo.

Track 18

Play the Dynamics

Playing with various dynamics and tempos can help the music sound expressive. Feel free to add these elements when you play music. Even "boring" exercises can sound musical with the use of dynamics and different rates of speed.

Up and Down

Remember, dynamic changes can be shown with the abbreviations *cresc.* for gradually getting louder and *dim.* for gradually getting softer. Make these changes with the amount of air you use.

Make the dynamic changes *gradual.* This will help your playing sound smooth.

Style Markings

A word or phrase will often appear above the staff in the upper, left-hand corner. It will help you play the music using the proper style. Words like **Expressively, Moderately, Gently** and **Flowing** will indicate the overall feel of the music. *Style markings* are just as important as tempos and dynamics when determining how a piece of music is to be played.

Look at the style marking for the next piece. Does it tell you how to play it?

Come On, Ev'rybody!

What dynamic level did you use? What was the tempo? Rock on!

D'lightful (New Note: D)

Do not cover the thumbhole for this note. Roll your left thumb slightly towards you and away from the hole. Use your right thumb to help balance the recorder.

₵ Time Signature: Common Time

Common time (₵) is the same as $\frac{4}{4}$.

Track 22

Scale the Mountain

The time signature of $\frac{4}{4}$ is so common that it is not hard to see why it is called "common time."

Try this experiment. Turn on your radio. Tap your foot to the beat of the music. Determine how many beats are grouped into measures. Does it sound like a quarter note equals one beat and they are in groups of four? Then the music would be written in $\frac{4}{4}$ or common time.

Music History

Having a sense of the origin for music can be very helpful. Whether it is the original country for a famous folk song, the era of a pop song and who recorded it, or the composer and title of a piece of classical music; it is all important information.

The next melody comes from a symphony written by Ludwig van Beethoven (1770–1827). Sometimes it is called "Ode to Joy" and is sung. It is from the fourth movement of Beethoven's *Ninth Symphony*. Play it with a sense of pride.

Track 23

Ode to Joy (from Symphony No. 9)

Further Study:

- How many symphonies did Beethoven write?
- What is another name for his *Ninth Symphony?*
- What medical ailment did Beethoven suffer?

- Balance the recorder with your left and right thumbs.
- Curve your fingers so the fleshy part of the fingertips cover the holes.

$\frac{2}{4}$ Time

A time signature of $\frac{2}{4}$ means that a quarter note gets one beat, but there are only two beats in a measure.

Track 24

Two by Two

Count/ **1 & 2 &   1 & 2 &   1 & 2 &   1 & 2 &   1 & 2 &   1 & 2 &   1 & 2 &   1 & 2 &**
Tap:

Skips

The previous song used notes that are not directly next to each other in pitch like G to B and D to G. These are called *skips*.

Fermata

The *fermata* (⌢) indicates that a note or rest is held somewhat longer than normal.

Track 25

Hold It!

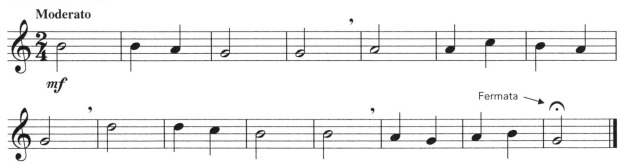

Steps

The previous song used notes that are directly next to each other in pitch like B to A and D to C. These are called *steps*.

Jingle Bells

Play with a joyous bounce without making it sound choppy. Hold the last note longer than two beats but with a controlled sound.

Can you find the skips and the steps? Draw a box around a skip. Draw a circle around a step. What note is played the most?

Phrase

A *phrase* is a musical "sentence," often 2 or 4 measures long. Try to play a phrase in one breath.

Aura Lee

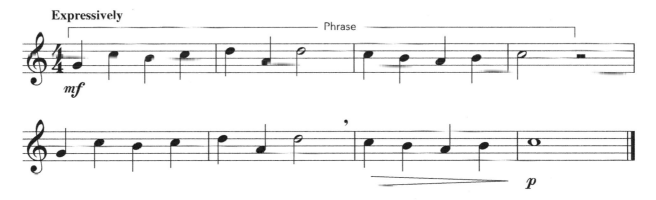

Hand and Finger Position

Now is a good time to go back to page 3 and review proper hand and finger position. This is very important for proper technique. Keeping the fingers curved and close to their assigned holes will allow your fingers and hands to be relaxed and will help in getting from one note to the next quickly, easily, and accurately. The further you lift your fingers off the holes, the more likely that you will put them down on the wrong hole or not completely close the hole. Besides that, fingers pointing in all directions doesn't look good!

Lightly Row

Identify the phrases. Put a breath mark at the end of each phrase. Can you play each phrase in one breath? Breath support is a good thing!

Posture

Good body posture will allow you to take in a full, deep breath and to control the air better as you play. Sit or stand with your spine straight and tall. Your shoulders should be back and relaxed. Keep your jaw parallel to the floor and don't let your right arm drop down. Think about your posture as you begin playing and check it several times.

Maryann in the Sand

Find a friend to play the chords on guitar or piano as you play the melody on the recorder. You can even add percussion instruments like shakers and bongos to help create an island atmosphere. Feel the cool, island breezes?

Is the melody mainly skips or steps? Which do you find more difficult to play and why?

Easy Street (New Note: E)

Add the first and second fingers of your right hand to the first
three fingers and thumb of your left hand to play this note.
Do not blow too hard to play this low note.

Japanese Flower Song

Play with long phrases. The tempo is not fast and should have the sense of moving forward.
By now your playing should sound musical – like you are singing through your recorder.

Lullaby

Here is your challenge: how softly can you play and still keep a steady tone with good sense of
pitch? This lullaby could be played late at night to help a baby go to sleep. You wouldn't want
to wake them up with a harsh sound, would you?!

Are you hearing the natural phrases in music? Do you take a breath at the end of each phrase?
Playing the recorder well takes musicianship and breath management.

Track 33

Rock 'n' Rests

Count like crazy for this next one! Even though only quarter and half rests are used, sometimes the counting of rests goes from one measure to the next. Play each note with confidence without over blowing (there is that word again). Good luck playing the last note at the correct time. Count, count, count!

Track 34

Down Row (New Note: D)

This note is fingered using your first three fingers of both hands and the thumb of your left hand. The ring finger of your right hand covers two small holes.

Track 35

On the Farm

The next song has a repeat sign at the end of four measures. Go back to the beginning when you reach the sign the first time. Play the first four measures again then go on to play the rest of the song.

Track 36

Jolly Nick

Here is another song where a friend can play the chords on guitar or piano. Add the sound of sleigh bells to create even more of a festive sound.

Pick-up Notes

Sometimes there are notes that come before the first full measure. They are called *pick-up notes*. Often, when a song begins with a pick-up measure, the note's value (in beats) is subtracted from the last measure. To play this song with a one beat pick-up, you count "1, 2, 3" and start playing on beat 4.

Track 37

My Dreydl

One beat pick-up note

Last measure has 3 beats, not 4

Play this song as someone spins a dreydl.

- As you finger the notes on your recorder, you can practice quietly by speaking the names of the notes, counting out the rhythms, or singing or whistling the pitches.
- Don't let your cheeks puff out when you play.

Notes and Rests

Eighth Note/Eighth Rest

An eighth note has half the value of a quarter note, that is, half a beat. An eighth rest means to be silent for half a beat. There are eight eighth notes or eight eighth rests in a 4/4 measure.

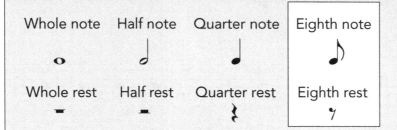

It is common to join two or more eighth notes with a beam (♫ or ♬). Individual eighth notes look like a quarter note with a flag on the stem (♪ or ♪).

Track 38

Eighth Note Jam

Count/ **1** & **2** & **3** & **4** & **1** & **2** & **3** & **4** & **1** & **2** & **3** & **4** & **1** & **2** & **3** & **4** &
Tap:

Eighth Note Counting

The first eighth note comes on "1" as your foot taps the floor. The second happens as your foot moves up on "&." The third is on "2" and the fourth is on the next "&" and so forth. Remember to count and tap in a steady and even manner, like the ticking of a clock.

Track 39

Down by the Station

Are you keeping track if your foot is up or down as you tap the beat and play eighth notes?

No Breath

There are times when you are **not** to take a breath. The phrase *no breath* will be written above the music.

Track 40

Hush Little Baby

Do not take a breath here → *no breath*

Track 41

Sharp Dresser (New Note: F♯)

Sharp Sign

A **sharp** sign (♯) raises the pitch a half step and remains in effect for the entire measure.

Raise the index finger on your right hand to play F♯.

Sharp sign

Track 42

Go Away, Rain

Moderato

Track 43

Oh, Susanna

Notice the pick-up notes.

23

Do Dah

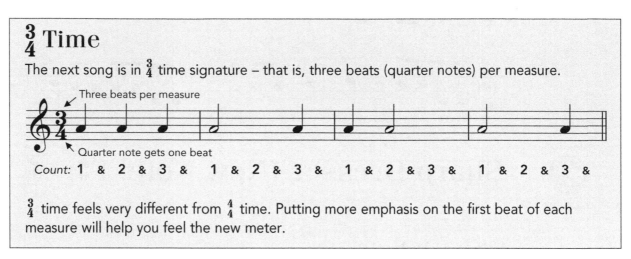

Three Beat Jam

Three to Get Ready

Morning (from Peer Gynt)

Tie

A *tie* is a curved line connecting two notes of the same pitch. It indicates that instead of playing both notes, you play the first note and hold it for the total time value of both notes.

= 2 beats

Track 48

Fit to Be Tied

Tie

Track 49

Alouette

Dot

A *dot* adds half the value of the note to which it is attached. A dotted half note (♩.) has a total time value of three beats:

| ♩. | – | ♩ | + | ♩ |
| Dotted half note (three beats) | | Half note (two beats) | | Quarter note (one beat) |

Therefore, a dotted half note has exactly the same value as a half note tied to a quarter note. Playing track 49 again, compare this music to the previous example:

Dot

1st and 2nd Endings

The use of **1st and 2nd endings** is a variant on the basic repeat sign. You play through the music to the repeat sign and repeat as always, but the second time through the music, skip the measure or measures under the "first ending" and go directly to the "second ending."

Mozart Variation

Accent

The **accent** (>) means you should emphasize the note to which it is attached. Do this by using a more explosive "d" on the "doo" with which you produce the note.

Up on a Housetop

William Tell

Notice the pick-up notes. Can you play the first six complete measures in one breath?

This Old Man

D.C. al Fine

At the **D.C. al Fine**, play again from the beginning, stopping at **Fine**. D.C. is the abbreviation for Da Capo *(dah cah' poh)*, which means "to the beginning." Fine *(fee' neh)* means "the end."

Banana Boat Song

A New Note: B♭ (B-flat)

Flat Sign

A *flat* sign (♭) lowers the pitch a half step.

Track 55

B-Flat Tune

Flat sign →

Natural Sign

A *natural* sign (♮) cancels a flat or a sharp for the remainder of the measure.

B-natural is the note you have been playing. Use the thumb and index finger of your left hand to play it.

Track 56

Be Natural

Natural sign →

Track 57

A New Note: F (F-natural)

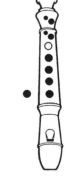

Up until now you have been playing F♯'s whenever a note was in the first space. Now you are to play F-naturals.

Andante

mf

Sea Chanty

Play B♭'s and F naturals in this song. Observe the dynamics and accent marks.

When the Saints Go Marching In

Key Signature – F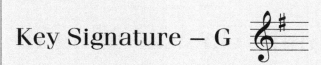

A **key signature** (the group of sharps and flats before the time signature) tells which notes are played as sharps and flats throughout the entire piece.

A key signature with one flat indicates that all written B's should be played as B♭'s. This is the **Key of F.**

Track 60

Skip to My Lou

Play F naturals and B♭'s throughout this song.

Key Signature – G

A key signature with one sharp indicates that all F's should be played as F♯'s. This is the **Key of G.**

Track 61

Home on the Range

Play all F's as F♯'s throughout this song.

Simple Gifts

Track 62

Moderately

mf

Sharps, Flats, and Naturals

Any sharp (♯), flat (♭), or natural (♮) sign that appears in the music but is not in the key signature is called an **accidental**. The accidentals in the next example are F♮ and B♭.

A **sharp** (♯) raises the pitch of a note by one half step.

A **flat** (♭) lowers the pitch of a note by one half step.

A **natural** (♮) cancels a previous sharp or flat, returning a note to its original pitch.

When a song requires a note to be a half step higher or lower, you'll see a sharp (♯), flat (♭), or natural (♮) sign in front of it. This tells you to raise or lower the note *for that measure only*. We'll see more of these "accidentals" as we continue learning more notes on the recorder.

Hard Rock Blues

Track 63

f

Track 64

Blues in G

Play any of these notes from the G blues scale to make up your own melody. Try playing patterns of notes using various rhythms.

12-Bar Blues in G

Here is the chord progression for a 12-bar blues in G. Have a friend play the chords on a guitar or piano as you improvise a melody. Some of the possible notes are included for your solo.

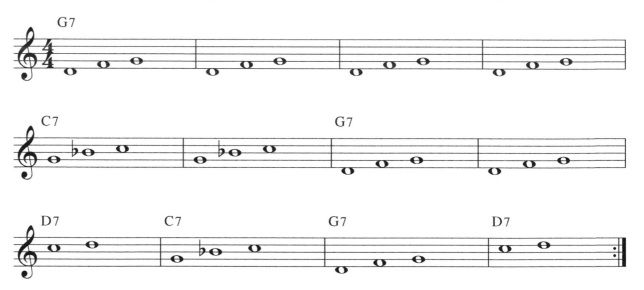

Congratulations! You have now completed *Play Recorder Today!*